Handbook of art activities

for primary-grade religion programs

by THEA EROES

William H. Sadlier, Inc.
New York, Chicago, Los Angeles

Contents

ISBN: 0-8215-5040-3
456789/9876543

THEME VI
The Christian life is life shared

SUPPLEMENTARY PROJECTS
Optional art projects

Helpful hints

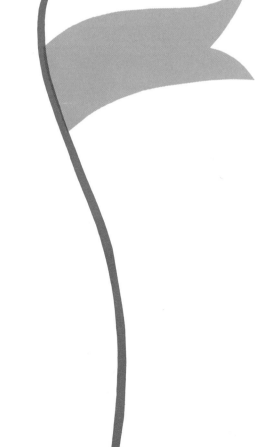

Why this book?

Its only purpose is to *help* the many generous people —
teachers, mothers, volunteers — who are seriously
interested in teaching religion to a new generation, who
can no longer be taught by formulas, memorized facts, or
mere textbooks. We need to help these people, who are
looking for creative ideas to make religion alive to the
children, creating a total experience for them, so that they
can become involved as whole persons, mentally and
physically, as well as emotionally. Art is the binding
force that unites a child's experiences and sensations. It
can become an outward manifestation of a very personal
religious experience. It is a meeting of the physical and the
spiritual in a beautiful inward relationship that only
through creative activity, as part of the religion lesson
plan, can take place inside the child and help him to grow
in love and in truth.

How to plan a lesson

1. Reduce your subject matter to one core theme.
   All projects in this book are based on a theme used in
   Grades 1-3. (But they could also be used in higher grades,
   deepening the given concept.) Most textbooks follow this
   thematic approach.
2. Always start a lesson with a sense experience or a familiar
   situation in a child's life. Gradually build on this
   experience to a related spiritual truth or value. This is
   done for you in this book as part of the art activity.
3. All art activity must be part of your lesson. It is never to
   be used by itself or tagged on as a "fill in." It is through
   the creative activity, as given here, that the child learns,
   experiences, and remembers the given concept.
4. Follow steps given under each project. Allow about 1 hour
   for each project. Motivation period is most essential; allow
   about five to ten minutes.
5. Have art material prepared in advance. (See basic
   procedure and materials.)
6. Know your children. Be interested in their background,
   their family relationship, and their age level in ability.
   Note: Detailed guidelines on the child's ability at various
   age levels is given in Sadlier's Creativity Kit: Tape and
   Slides.

Art terms and procedures

Room arrangement

1. Keep room as cheerful and informal as possible by moving desks or chairs into smaller groupings (if class is large), using floor area for informal seating on rugs or pillows.
2. Divide room into specific areas for variety and practicality.

   Work area: For creative projects, use tables or desks. (Pieces of plywood from a lumberyard placed on bricks can make fine tables. Old doors or wood crates can do the same.) Chairs are not always needed for work area. Children like to stand.

   Motivation area: A corner or book case, windowsill, or small table with books, pictures, magazines, and sense objects that children bring in is important for stimulating ideas.

   Records and record player are most useful here.

   Prayer area: With the children plan a place where the child can go to talk to God. Perhaps an open Bible or other symbol could make it a special place. Use it for prayer time for the group as well.

Art material, storage

1. *Individual*: Child should keep basic supplies in a shoe box or manila envelope. If possible keep in school so that it is always available. Store on shelf, under desks, or in makeshift stacked orange crates.

   Contents of shoe box: crayons, markers, scissors, paste, odds and ends. Optional: cray-pas, paint set, and small can.
2. *Teacher*: Keep certain supplies to facilitate preparation and distribution, as well as economy. Content of group box: all drawing and colored construction paper; clay; chalks; crystal tissue; tape; shelf paper for group projects; leftover seeds, glitter, etc. Optional: Poster paints, India ink, sprays, and fixatives.

Art materials, distribution

1. *Work area*: Should be covered with newspapers that can easily be cleaned up at end of period.
2. *Water*: If used, should be kept in large coffee cans (only half full if there are tables); place cans on paper plates.

   Individual desks: Each child has small empty juice can, lid completely removed. Keep water in empty Clorox bottles, and fill individual cans half full. Empty cans in a pail when finished.

   Note: Children of all ages can learn to handle this. Individual desks should be covered with newspapers as well.

Art materials, how to use

Crayons
Box of 12-16 colors sufficient.
Use point for fine details, but also *encourage other usage* of crayons.
Break crayon in half, peel paper off, and use the side, excellent for texture, large area background, and free movement.
Press hard for *waxy effect*. Crayons point may break off — do not make an issue of it. Neatness is not a criterion for good work. Freedom of expression is the aim.

Chalk
Use as crayon, point as well as side.
Break chalks in half before distribution, to avoid waste.
Keep chalks on paper plates, or in box tops, to avoid dropping on floor.

Markers
Use mostly wide, stubby kind. Try to get refillables for economy (see list of supply stores).
Be sure tops of markers are replaced to avoid drying out.
Black is essential, other colors optional.

Cray-pas
(Optional) A dry oil-color stick (not messy). Gives excellent colors, easy to handle, nice variety from crayon. (See supplementary art projects section.)

Paste
Keep tubes of paste or plastic jars in shoe box for individual use. For special projects only use Elmer's or other liquid glue. Keep in general supply box. Clean off nozzle with wet cloth after use. Can be refilled. Comes in economical gallon size. (See supply list.) Apply sparingly to backs of cutout shapes.

Scissors
Use rounded-point scissors only, for safety. One for each child. Keep in general box, or in individual boxes.

Paints
Simplest to use are watercolor trays, which include brushes. Worthwhile investment. One tray lasts for a long time, can be refilled, is easy to distribute, and there is no messy cleanup. Excellent for large groups. One to a child. Clean with paper towel between lessons to last longer; for water, see distribution.

Art terms, glossary

Abbreviations used
2-D=Two dimensional: shapes that are pasted down flat on a background.
3-D=Three dimensional: everything that stands up.

Banners
Any shape or material that can either be hung on a wall or carried in a parade or procession. Attach sticks of wood or heavy cardboard to ends of material.

Collage
Comes from the French *coller,* to paste. Any project where a number of shapes, pictures, or materials are arranged on a background and pasted down flat. No predrawing necessary. Arrange freely.

Mobile
Shapes, which should be made by individual children, hung with thin string to a basic frame. Frame hangs free from ceiling or twine. Moves freely when near door or window.
Basic frame: Use two sticks of equal length (36 inches), depending on size, or unbend two wire clothes hangers. Cross unbent wires and tape firmly in the middle.
Unbend a third hanger or piece of wire. Attach to center of crossed bars at one end. Bend the other end into a hook for hanging from ceiling fixture, water pipes, or twine that has been stapled between window or door frames.
Hang shapes from ends of crossed sticks first, to keep balance; add more gradually, keeping sticks balanced evenly.

Mosaic
The shapes pasted down here are more regular in size and form. Create a pattern by use of repetitious color, texture, or design. Outlines are drawn first; small shapes of paper (or other material) fill in predrawn design.

Mural
Group project in which each child draws, cuts, or paints a small part. All parts assembled together on a large background area create a picture, text, or desired decoration.

1 period
Usually 45-60 minutes (Do not rush projects. Take longer if necessary.)

Where to get materials

General school supply store
Basic bulk supplies (cheaper); crayons, drawing paper, assorted colored construction paper, scissors, paste, paint sets (8 colors and brush), markers; Crystal Craft and Clayola (usually)

Hardware stores or paint stores
All shellac sprays and fixative, gold spray (and other colors), sandpaper, plaster of paris, tape, string, Elmer's glue in large bottle, old wallpaper sample books (free)

Stationery stores
Colored markers, if you wish (only black is necessary); large-size wrapping paper and poster board for group projects; pipe cleaners, glitter, staplers.

Lumberyard
Wood stocks, for flag, balloons, banners, etc.; sand paper, Elmer's glue in gallon size (usually), woodscraps.

Supermarket
Balloons, paper plates, paper cups, transparent tape, stars, pasta shapes, seeds (corn peas, etc.), silver and gold wrapping paper (at Christmas), odds and ends.

Woolworth or local store
Sewing trims, glitter, styrofoam shapes, wool, felt squares, stickers, odds and ends.

Home throwaways
Boxes, ribbons, string, gift paper, buttons, etc.; old stockings, socks, paper bags, scrap material.
Note: Before throwing anything out, think, could I use it?
Example: Styrofoam from packing case of TV or other appliances.
Let children help you collect these items, keep in shoe box or in a box marked general. Always keep leftovers from a project. Many items can be used for a variety of projects.

Myself, a very special person God made

Basic concept

 Getting to know myself, who I am, who made me and loves me. Man reflects God's goodness in a special way. By looking at myself and at those around me I get to know something about God and His relationship to me. These projects aim to deepen the young child's awareness of and delight in differences expressed by individuals — by the way they look, by the things they like to do.

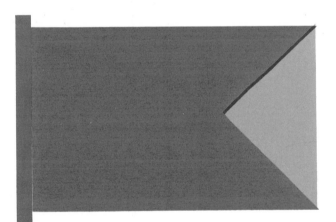

Project 1
Drawing myself

Motivation
We are all different; at the same time we are all created by God and, therefore, have much in common.

Materials
Mirror, either large one for an entire group or individual small ones for each child

Polaroid camera (if available) to take a picture of each child in class

OR Snapshot — You could ask the children to bring in one of themselves from home

Music or song:

Example: "Getting to know you"

Drawing paper 8 inches by 12 inches or larger

Crayons or markers

Procedure
Let children look at themselves and at each other.

Have them feel their own faces and name the basic shapes as they touch and then draw each part.

Example: Feel roundness of head. . .draw head. Feel longness of nose. . .draw nose. Continue until face is finished.

Add individual characteristics like hair (short or long), glasses, freckles, etc.

Encourage large drawing. Help children write their own names (Grade 1).

Let children now add to their drawings things they like to eat or play with, or part of their friends and family, whatever distinguishes them from the others.

Conclusion
Mount or simply tape pictures onto wall or colored background. Let children discuss each other's work. Cover up names; have children try to recognize each other. Can be used as a game of getting to know each other better.

Project 2
Mask
Variation of face project

Motivation
Same as for face drawing.

Add how I feel and express moods that are inside of me.

Example: happy=smile; sad=tears; anger=frown; etc.

Materials
Paper plate or drawing paper

Crayons, markers, staplers

Colored construction paper (mixed colors), thin string

Odds and ends of wool, string, buttons, etc. (if desired)

Procedure
Discuss moods with the children and how our faces change accordingly.

Child picks the mood he wishes to show.

Draws his face on inside of paper plate, using entire circle area. When drawing paper is used, make large circle first, draw inside circle.

Note: Keep circles large, features BIG.

Colors in features.

Adds hair and other details with colored paper, string, etc., or just draw details with crayon and markers.

Conclusion
Fasten string with stapler to sides of plate or paper. Tie around child's head.

Let children make several faces of different moods. Let them put on the different moods and tell you when and how they feel when they put on a particular mood.

Note: Excellent for playacting, by which the teacher gets to know children better and children become less inhibited with each other as well.

Keep masks displayed or in project folder for later use.

Project 3
Balloon faces

Motivation
Same as Project 1.

Materials
Balloons, small round ones preferred
Markers only (crayon will burst balloon)
Paste, heavy yarn (optional)
Paper cup or wood stick (optional)

Procedure
Draw face (as in project I and II) with marker on blown-up balloon. (Tie string to balloon after blowing it up to medium size. This facilitates handling.) Use marker lightly.
Decorate with yarn and paste (older children only).
Attach finished balloon to a stick with tape (Grades 1 & 2), or cut paper cup in half and tape balloon to upper half of paper cup so balloon can stand in place (Grade 3 & up only).

Conclusion
Can be used in a parade or as desk place marker.

Project 4
Face collage

Motivation
Basically the same. Perhaps more detailed attention should now be given to child's likes in food, clothing, toys, people, etc.

Materials
Life magazines (at least one to a child)
Drawing paper, crayons, markers, scissors, paste

Procedure
Grades 1 & 2
Draw large circle on paper.
Cut out from magazine pictures of things child likes.
Paste inside circle close together, overlapping desirable. Leave no spaces empty; pictures can be of different sizes.
Draw details of face over magazine pictures with marker, or simply have child write his name over collage.

Procedure
Grade 3 & up
Draw profile of face if a variation is desirable. Let child feel his face with hand first, starting at top of head. Let him make a continuous movement over nose, mouth and chin. Repeat several times, until he feels when his face goes in and when it protrudes out.
Cut magazine pictures and paste inside profile outline.
Add details with marker.
Contrasting paper from magazine or lettering from magazine can be used to write name under or across face.

Conclusion
Mount collages on contrasting paper individually or on large strip of wallpaper. Display in room.
Grades 1 & 2: Can write title for display such as: I Am Someone Special, or God Made Me Special.
Grade 3 & up: Each child can write something about himself and paste it under his picture (on separate paper).
Display of this face "gallery" is very popular. Can be used as part of spontaneous prayers for each other at end of lesson, or in later lessons if a child is sick or has a particular concern.
This leads into projects in THEME II *when the child realizes more deeply that we need each other.*

Project 5
Name pendant

Basic concept

What is a name? Why do people and things have names? Giving a name to a toy or a pet makes it part of my world, makes it special. There are symbols in names. Discuss and discover some with your children.

Names help people to know each other. God gave us each a name. This concept should gradually be built up to a better understanding of Baptism, where as a child of God a name symbolizes the person's acceptance into the Church, the family of God.

Motivation

Discuss the importance of a name.

Play a game of name identification. (See who knows the names of all the children in the group.) Find out the symbols of some of the names.

Materials

Cardboard, oak tag, poster paper, or cardboard boxes

Variety of pasta shapes from supermarket: pasta bows, shells, macaroni

Thin spaghetti

Variety of seeds or grains like beans, corn, peas. (One package of each kind is sufficient for 50 children.)

Paper cups or small box tops

Thin cord, as for parcels

Paste, scissors and assorted sizes of empty cans

Gold spray (not to be handled by children) or thick paint

Newspaper to cover work area

Procedure

Trace bottom of can on the cardboard with a pencil. Keep shape large. *Repeat the identical shape.* Each child should have two shapes of same size.

Cut circles out with scissors. (For first graders it may be necessary to precut circles if cardboard is too heavy.)

Place each kind of shape in a paper cup or box top for easier handling.

Paste spaghetti or cord in the middle of circle, forming initials of name or whole name. Some children will draw letters first with pencil, then paste, others prefer to form and paste letters directly.

Decorate the remaining part of the circle with shapes of their choice. (Avoid overcrowding shapes.)

Let dry for five minutes. During this time children work on second shape.

Second shape procedure the same. This time *let child decide* what he wishes to put inside circle.

Suggestion: a friend's name, God's name, a symbol of Baptism or other religious meaning.

Spray circles, with decorations firmly pasted on, with gold spray. This should be done on a separate table covered with newspaper. Spray should be handled by teachers for younger children.

OR Paint circles. Let children choose own color. When dry, shellac. This procedure takes more time than spraying.

Sparkles can be added with a little paste when spray is dry. Older children enjoy this added touch of color. (Younger children are too anxious to wear pendants right away.)

Paste finished circles together, back to back.

Punch a small hole at the top of pendant.

Cut cord long enough to go around child's neck. Put cord through hole and the child is ready to wear the pendant.

Conclusion

Aim of lesson: God has left a special mark of identification on each of us by making us His child at Baptism. We are marked by His love. We can show that we are Christians by exterior signs also. Make this a basis for discussion and draw simple examples according to age and capacity of child.

Example: How do I live as a child of God?

Let wearing the pendant express certain inward attitudes as well: love, friendship, etc.

Close with a prayer or song, like: "They'll Know We Are Christians by Our Love."

I am part of a group

Basic concept

God has placed man in groups as a member of family, country, church. We must work out our salvation in relation to others. We cannot live alone. We need each other. Each person reflects God's love in a special way. Only by sharing this love with others can we truly give honor and glory to God.

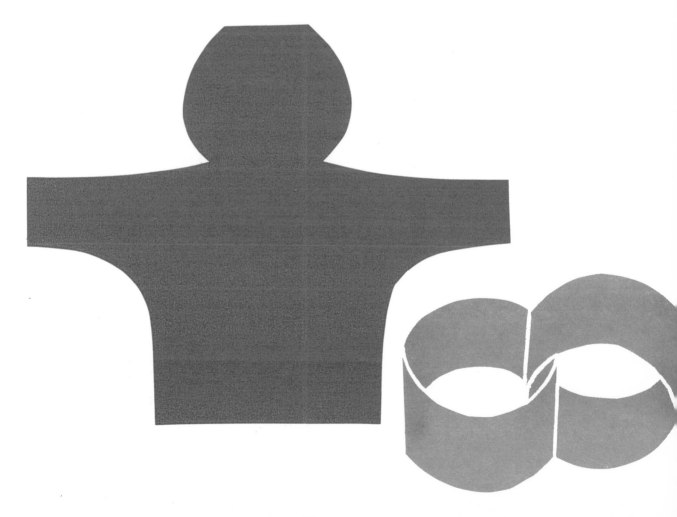

Project 6
Finger puppets

Motivation
Help children to become conscious of the needs of others. Let each tell of an incident where they needed help and how they got it (stress family unit, making friends).
Sense experience: Use game or song.

Materials
White drawing or construction paper, 8"x12"
Scissors, paste, crayon
Stapler or rubberbands
Odds and ends left over from previous activity

Procedure
Fold 8 inch by 12 inch paper in half, making a crease. Place folded paper in front of you with crease at the top.

Draw figure of puppet on folded paper, making sure the top of the head touches the crease. Use entire paper for figure. (See Fig. 6a.)

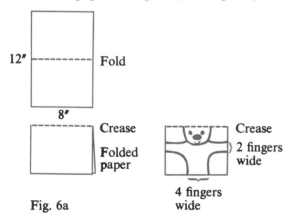

Fig. 6a

Note: First graders may experience difficulties with this. If so, prestencil shape for them if necessary. Older children can draw this themselves, if you give them a few pointers. Such as:
   Use capital U for head, touching crease.
   Arms should be two fingers wide.
   Body should be four fingers wide.
Insist on measuring with their fingers; otherwise they tend to make shapes too small and skinny for use later on.

Cut out shape following drawn outline. Take care to hold both top and bottom paper together when cutting. Do not cut top of U, so that the two pieces remain attached only at the head.

Paste outside edges together, or staple for younger children. Leave bottom open so finger can slip in.

Decorate. Each child is free now to make the basic puppet shape into a person: himself, his friend, or a member of his family. More puppets can be added as time allows.

Decoration hints: Younger children can use crayons or markers for face and clothing. Older children enjoy more elaborate clothing and details with colored construction paper, using wool or string for hair.

Conclusion
Puppet is placed on finger. Each child can introduce his puppet to the rest of the group. Let the puppet make friends with another puppet. Encourage playacting. This project can be prolonged over one or more lessons. Older children delight in making the whole family, or their circle of friends. One child can have several finger puppets on both hands and so create a whole story by himself or herself. Listen to the conversation to get to know the child better. Pick up words or feelings that the children express and relate them to a religious concept, such as: There is joy in sharing our life with others, as God enjoys sharing His life and love with us.

Project 7
Paper links
to form a chain

Motivation
To extend the children's awareness of belonging together in a group and to foster class spirit, you might like to discuss a slogan, scripture text, or simple concept that will be the identifying theme for your group during the year.

Younger children might choose just words. Older ones like to paraphrase secular sayings, i.e., GOD POWER or THINGS GO BETTER WITH GOD.

Materials
Mixed colored construction paper
Paste, scissors, crayons, or markers
Staplers

Procedure
Make basic link by either precutting two-inch-wide strips about six to eight inches long or letting older children measure and cut strips themselves.

Cut one or more strips two inches wide and about eight inches long.

Draw with crayon, each child writing his name on a strip and decorating it in any manner he wishes.

Paste is placed at the outer ends of each strip.

Each strip is linked to the next by pasting ends of strips together, interlocking each strip. (See Fig. 7a.)

Fig. 7a

Variations
The basic chain can be hung up across a room or along a wall.

1. The letters of the theme or slogan chosen by the group can be attached to the chain. Letters should be on a contrasting color paper, with each letter stapled or pasted onto a link. (See Fig. 7b.)

Fig. 7b

2. A photo of each child attached to the link with his name on it.
3. Older children enjoy making symbols or pictures depicting the different groups they belong to, such as family, school, church, community, city, etc., and attaching these to the links.

Conclusion
After proper display and discussion as to the meaning of the project, a song sung in a circle, linking hands, or an appropriate prayer could end this lesson.

Project 8
Flags and banners
Grades K-3

Motivation
To help the child experience the satisfaction that comes from sharing activities, he must experience many outward creative experiences as a member of a group. Planning a parade or prayer service, however simple, allows each child to make a distinct and valuable contribution. Try to relate this to the concept that the Church is a community of believers, and through our active participation we help to make God's presence in the world visible to others. Prepare by discussing plans with children, letting them contribute ideas for parade or prayer service. Play march music for parade or choose songs for prayer service. Discuss reasons for parades or processions. Plan theme for flags or banners.

Materials
Mixed colored construction paper
Wood sticks (from lumber yard)
Markers, chalks, crayons, odds and ends
Masking tape

Procedure
Each child chooses a colored piece of construction paper 8 by 12 inches.
Place on table with the shorter side near you (Fig. 8a).
Draw an upside down V at bottom (Fig. 8b) from corner to corner.
Cut out V-shape with scissors (Fig. 8c).

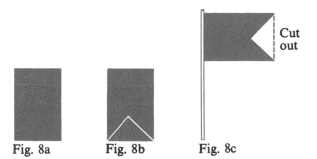

Fig. 8a   Fig. 8b   Fig. 8c

Turn paper with long side near you, and proceed with decorations.
Decoration possibilities:
Write in capital letters word expressing theme: JOY, LOVE, SHARE, etc.
Draw pictures of God, Jesus, or illustrate a Bible story.
Encourage large drawing and lettering, strong colors, filling entire flag on both sides.

Conclusion
Tape paper flag to one end of stick for child to carry in parade or procession.
Flags can also be strung across the room by stapling one side to a string suspended between walls. Ends of string also can be stapled or taped to wood frames of windows as decorations for prayer service or room.
Individual flags can be placed on the desk of each child when not carried. Form a large ball of modeling clay (play dough), place clay ball on a paper plate or box top, stick flag in clay ball.

Project 9
Banners
Grade 3 & up

Motivation

Same as for flag, perhaps deepening the concept of community and our union with Jesus as our friend and leader, helping us to praise the Father in communal worship.

Materials

Long pieces of colored shelf paper or burlap
Masking tape
Pieces of felt, scrap materials, or colored construction paper
Odds and ends of buttons, wool ends, sequins, glitter, trim
Elmer's glue, scissors, stapler
Pencil and scrap paper

Procedure

Plan: On scrap paper let small groups of children plan theme or words for their banner. About four or six children to one banner, depending on size of class. Restrict words to five or six to avoid overcrowding. Help children to space letters over entire area and not too close to edge.

Tape material or paper to a table so material is taut and does not move.

Cut desired shape and letters out of colored paper or felt. Keep them large so they can be seen from a distance.

Do not paste down too early. Let children arrange pieces first on paper or cloth. Only if entire banner design looks pleasing and well spaced, *then*:

Paste down all the pieces one by one. Do not remove them from the background while pasting. Simply hold piece down with one hand and slip paste underneath, careful not to move piece from appointed place.

Decorate — with trims, sequins, buttons, yarn — words of greater importance or symbols reinforcing the words. Do not overload the banner. A few well-placed trims can go a long way for effect.

Attach wooden stick (broom end, windowshade stick, or piece from lumberyard) to top and bottom end of paper or material with stapler. Tie wool or string to each end of top stick (Fig. 9a).

Fig. 9a

Conclusion

Banner can be displayed in room or on door. It can be hung in church at the children's prayer or worship service.

Project 10
My Church

Motivation

Make a visit to your church or place of worship. Discuss why it is important to set aside a certain place and time for prayer and worship. Stress the importance of common prayer as a form of acknowledgment of God's presence in the life of the Christian community. Take children around church, show them where children are Baptized; tell them how they became part of the Christian community.

Materials

Colored construction paper
Scissors and crayons or markers, paste, stapler

Procedure

Grades 1 & 2

Take a sheet of 8 by 12 inch paper with short side near you. This is the basic shape of a building.

Take a second sheet of paper and *draw* a large triangle from corner to corner. (See Figs. 10a & 10b.)

Cut the triangle out.

Paste the triangle as a roof on top of the first paper. (See Fig. 10c.)

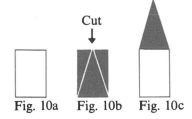

Fig. 10a   Fig. 10b   Fig. 10c

Decorate: Children add details of building (such as windows, doors, name of church) and other markings (bell, cross, etc.). If desired, children can use back side to draw what they saw inside of church.

Variation

Grade 3 & up

Use a shoe box or milk carton as basic 3-D shape of building.

Cover with construction paper or paint outside with tempera paints. (See instruction for painting.)

With markers, crayons, or paint, add details.

Back of box can be cut open to reveal inside of church if desired.

Conclusion

If several periods are used for this theme, it may be interesting to let the children plan a whole community of buildings. Same procedure is used as above for 2-D or 3-D project. Add homes, school, stores, post office. If 2-D is used, tape buildings next to each other in room or hallway so they form a street; add people. Title suggestion: "The Christian Community." If 3-D is used, place on table or on window sill, forming a village. Add people and details as you and your group wish.

Details of 3-D people will be found in Project 24, "Christmas Figures."

Plan a prayer corner in your room, using the buildings.

Project 11
Murals: hands

Motivation

We need each other to be happy.

Explore the way all creatures are dependent on one another. All living things are bound together by the way they interact on each other. Help the child experience the satisfaction that comes from sharing activities.

Sense activity: Find and discuss photos from magazines and books about animals and people and how they need each other. Let children tell you when and how they received help at times, play a game, or act out a situation where we help each other using *hands*.

Materials

Individual drawing paper for Grade 1

Colored construction paper for older children

Long piece of shelf paper (light color)

Tape scissors, paste, crayons, markers

Procedure

Grades 1 & 2

Draw or trace own hand on drawing paper with crayon or marker. If cutting out the drawn hand is difficult, finish it as a picture only.

Color with crayon, write own name, then add other hands of those who help him.

Example: parents, teacher, God.

Older children

Cut out the drawn hand.

Tape long shelf paper to a wall or on a table.

Color hands as child desires. Words can be written on hands and fingers, showing what we use hands for: sharing, friendship, love, caring, etc.

Grade 3 & *up*

Add with crayon, or cut out of colored paper, objects that one gives to help others.

Examples: food, clothing, money, sharing toys, candy, etc.

Paste: arrange hands on long shelf paper. Place larger shapes first, smaller can overlap if necessary. Let children take turns (a few at a time only) pasting hands and object down. (Hands should point in different directions.)

Words written with markers or cutout letters from darker colored construction paper can be superimposed if desired.

Note: Sample of this found in creativity kit, tape and slides.

Variation

Eyes

"To see the need of others"

Cut out eyes from magazines (part of face only), OR Draw eyes. . .choose eyes of different colors, different racial backgrounds, different kinds of expressions.

Arrange and paste as in hand project.

Make any additions that may be suggested by the children.

Mouth

"To speak the Word of God, or to spread the Good News"

Draw or cut pictures of mouths from magazine (same as above).

Add Scripture texts or any other symbols of communication.

Ears

"Ears to hear the Word of God and do it"

Same procedure as above.

Project 12
Heart mobile

Motivation

Basically the same motivation as Project 11. Extend now to more interior, spiritual sharing, such as love through sacrifice, giving of oneself. Bible stories of Jesus and how He showed His love for us can be a basis for this project.

Materials

Red construction paper

Odds and ends like silver foil, fancy paper from gift wraps, ribbons, glitter, paper doilies, or trims (ask children to collect and bring)

Paste, scissors, crayons or markers

Procedure

(Teacher should work along with children, do step by step with them. The actual work should be done by the children.)

Fold 8½ by 11 inch red construction paper in half (Fig. 12a). Keep folded, place closed booklet in front of you with crease on *left side*. (Make sure of this.)

Draw half a heart on fold with crayon or marker (Fig. 12b), keeping shape large.

Folded—
crease left

Fig. 12a   **Fig. 12b**

Cut, holding both pieces of paper together. Do not cut on fold.

Open heart and decorate with pictures, symbols, fancy paper, as desired.

Grade 1

May stop here. Either paste heart on a different colored paper or hang around neck (like pendant) with "I love God" on one side, and "God loves me" on the other. Any variation here that ties in with your lesson can be used.

Mobile

See section on mobiles (page 8) for basic instructions.

Attach thin string or heavy thread to cutout heart shapes with transparent tape or stapler.

Tie strings to crossed sticks or wire (about 10-12 hearts to one mobile). String can be of different lengths. (See Fig. 12c.)

Fig. 12c

Conclusion

Hang mural or mobile where the whole group can see it or share project with other children and parents.

Do not remove too soon. Later lessons can tie in with this basic theme; and by referring to this project, the children will be able to recall the lesson more readily.

THEME III
God's gifts to me

Section 1
Creation

Basic concept

God's presence can be discovered in creation. Explore the need we have for all of God's creations. All men are dependent on God's creations: air, sun, water, plants, and animals. All of these are only signs of a much greater gift from God. His greatest gift is His only Son, Jesus.

Project 13
Thank you God book

Motivation

To explore God's creation for reflections of His goodness. By seeing, touching, and smelling various facets of creation, children can gain greater understanding of God and His goodness.

Sense activities: The younger child, especially, discovers the world around him through his senses. Older children need to be made freshly aware of the variety and beauty of God's gifts to man.

1. Have children bring in different objects from nature.
2. Focus on really *seeing* by asking them to name or write ten things they discover about the objects they brought in.

   Note: The teacher may bring in a few objects with different textures or shapes to give children plenty of variety; i.e., flowers, leaves, stones, shells, bark of trees, salt, sugar, peppercorns, fruits, vegetables, etc.

3. Use a whole period for this. Always relate to a God concept:

   Seeing. . .Jesus likened faith to the ability to see.

   Touching. . .Jesus expressed God's saving power through His use of touch. Use Gospel story to illustrate this.

   Food. . .Food extends child's senses of taste and smell. Enjoyment of these associated to God's goodness. Jesus uses food to show how God cares for us.

Materials

Collected objects of small size or parts of larger ones dried between paper and heavy books in period 1 (if applicable), cardboard or colored construction paper, crayons, markers, paste, scissors.

Procedure

Grade 1

Paste or tape objects onto cardboard, making a pleasing arrangement, according to child's wishes.

Print a title with marker, such as "God's Gifts to Me" or any other words, expressing "Thank You God," the core message of the lesson.

Grade 2 & up

Tape one object to each sheet of colored paper. Take as many sheets as objects, no less than five.

Write next to or under each object what it teaches you about God.

Form into a booklet, using last empty page for a poem or prayer that the children make up themselves about God's goodness as manifested to them through these gifts.

Staple pages together, using another empty page as a title page. Encourage children to draw and decorate title page any way they like, giving it their own title expressing the idea of "My Book of God's Gifts to Me," "Thank You God Book," etc.

Conclusion

Display booklets, or let children keep in their project folders. Use occasionally as part of your prayer time. May be used as a form of litany or related to a psalm used for a prayer service.

Project 14
Burlap and felt banner

Motivation
Same as Project 13

Materials
Burlap
Assorted felt squares (See section on materials.)
Heavy yarn
White chalk
Scissors
Wooden sticks

Procedure
Cut burlap into individual pieces, about 15 inches wide by 20-25 inches long.
Tape a piece of burlap to table surface in front of each child.
Write on blackboard different kinds of fruits and vegetables the children like, discussing basic shapes.
Examples: round for apple, long for banana, etc.
Let children select different colored felt. One larger piece can be kept for bowl or table top (use last). On the smaller pieces (approximately 5 inches square) let each child draw with chalk the fruit or vegetable he wishes. One object to each square piece of felt. (See Fig. 14a.)

 5-inch square felt

Fig. 14a

Note: encourage large shapes. If first try is not successful, erase chalk drawing with hand, or use reverse side of felt square; do not waste felt.
Cut out shapes. (First graders may have difficulties cutting felt.) If group is small, give individual help. If group is large, precut geometric shapes only (i.e. circles, triangles, squares), and let children put shapes together to form desired objects.

Place shapes in center of burlap piece, placing larger shapes first, smaller overlapping larger ones. Encourage grouping shapes so they connect with each other. Also, move them around freely so they do not always stand right up "like soldiers." (See Fig. 14b.)

Fig. 14b

Paste with Elmer's glue to burlap. Heavy yarn can be added for extra texture, outline, or words (sample of this in Creativity Kit, tape and slides). Finished banner should be attached to stick with glue or staples.
Tie yarn to stick ends for hanging. Bottom of burlap can be taped to a second stick or fringed.

Conclusion
Children enjoy taking this project home, hanging it in a special place where it can be seen by all, as a reminder to thank God for all the food and gifts He gives us each day. A meal prayer could be learned.
Example: For food and drink and all good things we give You thanks, O Lord.

Project 15
A festive meal...joy shared

Motivation
A family feast is a reflection of the heavenly banquet. Here on earth we express our communal joy with feasts and celebrations. The Thanksgiving feast here in the United States should have an extra dimension for us as Christians, expressing our gratitude and love for all God has done for us.

Sense experience: Let children bring in cookies or bread, grapes or juice. Experience the joy of sharing food. Make it festive with decorations, party hats, favors; have a class party.

Relate to the Last Supper, when Jesus shared the most precious moments of His life with those He loved so dearly.

Materials
Grade 1
Drawing paper, crayons or paints (see section on painting), chalks or markers.

Procedure
Take 8 by 12 inch drawing paper.
Fold in half.
Open and draw two pictures (one in each section)
One half: Thanksgiving meal, the child and his family seated at a table with food.
Other half: Last Supper, Jesus and His Apostles. (See Fig. 15a.)

Thanksgiving meal | | Last Supper

Fig. 15a

Conclusion
Write title or prayer expressing joy in sharing God's life through celebrations.

Grade 2 & up
Individual drawings, as above or *group project mural.*

Mural materials
Large paper (sheet of wrapping paper, largest size)
Colored chalk or paints
Colored construction paper
Scissors
Paste

Procedure
Divide large paper into two sections (same as above).
Select a few children who volunteer to draw background on large paper (tape paper to wall or floor)
Divide children in their seats into groups of 2 or 3 to draw and cut out chosen subjects.
Examples:
  Group 1 – *people* (child and family for Thanksgiving side, Jesus and Apostles for other side)
  Group 2 – *fruits and food* for tables.
Note: if group is large, subdivide into smaller groupings.
Children who work on background should fill in large areas, such as floor, walls, tables, windows, decorations.
When all are finished with their respective work, have children who cut out shapes paste them in their proper places.

Conclusion
Hang up mural in room, hallway, or place of worship used for background of Thanksgiving service or puppet plays.

God's gifts to me

Section 2
We prepare for His coming

Basic concept

God's greatest gift to us is His Son Jesus. We became brothers
of Christ through Baptism. In Baptism Christ chose us and
we chose Him. We grow in His friendship by getting to
know Jesus better and by imitating those who prepared for
His coming before His birth. We, too, must prepare for His
birth at Christmas each year, for Jesus did not only come
in history a long time ago; He comes to us today as well,
through His love, into our hearts if we are open to Him.
We also look forward to His coming at the end of time, for
which our life here is a form of preparation.

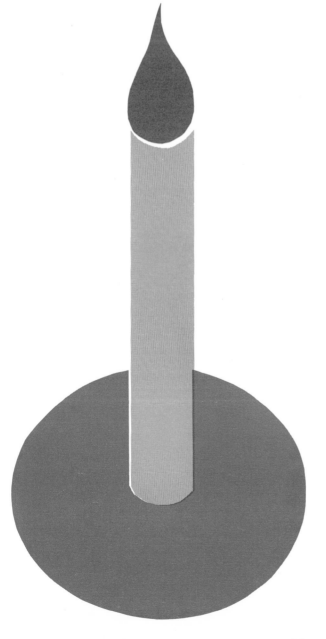

Project 16
Saying yes to God
Mural, booklet

Motivation

As Mary was chosen by God to play a special role in the life of Jesus, so we, too, are chosen by God to fulfill a mission. Mary was willing to let herself be used by God, by saying yes to His will for her.

We must be open to what God wants of us, and say yes to His will for us as well.

Sense activity: Read or act out story with puppets.

Grades 1 & 2

How Mary said yes to God. When and how we say yes to God in our daily lives.

Grade 3 & *up*

Take other people from Old or New Testament who accepted God's will, however hard it was.

Examples: Abraham, Moses, Peter, Paul, etc.
Contemporaries: Martin Luther King, President Kennedy, etc.

Materials

Large paper taped to wall or floor
Colored construction paper
Chalk, crayons, or paints
Glitter, paste, scissors

Procedure

Draw and cut large triangle from 8 by 12 inch construction paper.

Each child draws picture on triangle of either a person from Scripture who said yes, or himself or herself saying yes to God.

Examples: Abraham said yes. (Name of child) said yes.

Draw and cut large circle of yellow construction or shelf paper for center.

Paste circle in middle of paper (symbol of God: no beginning, no end). (See Fig. 16a.)

Fig. 16a

Paste finished triangles around center circle.

Cut up leftover colored paper from triangles into small pieces.

Each child *pastes* a small piece of this paper into center circle, signifying we are all part of God's life when we do His will.

Note: Slide of this project in Creativity Kit.

Conclusion

A short prayer like:

"Lord, let me grow to be that for which You have destined me,"

OR an appropriate psalm.

Project 17
Advent posters announce His coming

Motivation
Any important visitor must be welcomed after detailed preparations are made for His arrival. Discuss situations from familiar happenings: the visit of a president or astronaut, or a local dignitary; preparations at home when a special visitor is coming. Jesus wants to come into our hearts in a very special way at Christmas, so we must prepare for this event, not only outwardly with decorations but inwardly as well.

Materials
Construction paper, scissors, paste, ruler, pencil, crayons or markers.

Procedure
Discuss and list words that will help us prepare for His coming to announce to others who is coming and why.

Let the children choose one of the words.

Example: prepare, waiting, coming, joy, advent, etc.

Take a sheet of 8 by 12 inch construction paper the long way (Fig. 17a).

Fig. 17a

With ruler, draw lines one inch apart from top to bottom of the paper. (Younger children may take the width of the ruler as guide.)

Cut strips apart with scissors.

Take a long sheet of shelf paper, or paste together three sheets of construction paper; *make a strip* about 36 inches long.

Place inch-wide strips on paper to form capital letters (Fig. 17b).

Fig. 17b

Paste down when satisfied with spacing.

Draw in between letters to illustrate Christ's coming.

Example: about the three comings:
Crib, without child
Heart, ways of preparing, prayer, sacrifice
Coming in glory

Other symbols or pictures may be used as desired.

Conclusion
These posters make nice wall decorations in classroom.

Use as posters around school or community to remind others of the spiritual aspect of Christmas.

Project 18
Light comes into darkness

Motivation

The necessity and purpose of light in our lives. Scripture and liturgy use the symbol of light as a sign of God's presence in the world and in us (baptismal candle, lights in church, symbol of the candle, etc.).

Sense experience: Darken the room, let the children feel darkness by closing eyes. Divide the children into four groups representing the four corners of the earth. Each group stands in one of the corners of the room. After standing in the darkness for some time and asking God, the Light of the World, to come to them and to the world, light a candle in the middle of the room. Appropriate songs, or prayers can be used to begin or end session as children unite around the candle. Older children could be given candles, which they light from this central Christ candle. They then return to their respective corners with the light they have received from the Christ candle.

2-D candle
Materials

Grades 1 & 2
Dark color construction paper
Silver or gold paper (white or yellow can also be used)
Green and red construction paper
Sparkles
Paste, scissors, crayons

Procedure

Cut a strip of gold or silver paper two inches wide, six inches long.
Paste on dark construction paper, so that enough room is left at the top for flame. Use construction paper the long way. Draw and cut a flame out of yellow paper (an O with a point). (See Fig. 18a.)

Fig. 18a

Paste flame above strip for candle, leaving a little space for wick.
Draw wick with black marker or crayon, or cut from paper.
Decorate candle with sparkles.

Draw decorations at bottom of candle, like holly leaves (described in 3-D candle project).
Bows out of ribbon or wool ends may be added.
Print words or short prayers with crayons or markers.
Examples: Enlighten our hearts. Give light to the world. Increase the light of faith in us.

3-D candle
Materials

Grades 2, 3, *up*
Paper plate
Cardboard tube (from paper towels)
Silver foil or shiny Christmas paper (any color)
Green, yellow, or black construction paper
Scissors, paste, staplers or tape
Pencil, markers, crayons
Odds and ends, such as ribbons, bows, wool yarn, glitter

Procedure

Cover cardboard tube with foil or colored paper. Paste ends down, so paper is fastened firmly around tube.
Cut into base of candle short snips about one half inch deep at one-inch intervals (Fig. 18b).

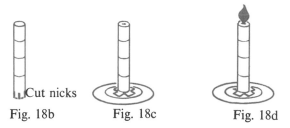

Cut nicks

Fig. 18b   Fig. 18c   Fig. 18d

Bend tabs outward, put paste on each tab.
Paste or staple down on paper plate (Fig. 18c).
Cut three-inch long strip of paper, one inch wide. If preferred, older children cut circle a little larger than opening of tube, and paste on top (Fig. 18d).
Draw and cut out flame. (See instruction for 2-D candle.)
Cut slit into candle on strip that covers top of tube.
Insert flame, tape or paste to make secure.

Holly leaves

Decorate base of candle with *holly leaves* if
desired: Fold green construction paper in half
(Fig. 18f). Fold again to make piece four by
six inches. Draw with white chalk one large
holly leaf (Fig. 18g). Cut out, keeping paper
folded; this will make four large leaves. Cut
out small red circles for berries. Paste leaves
over tabs of tube. Paste red berries as desired
on leaves.

Finish by adding sparkle or ribbons as desired.

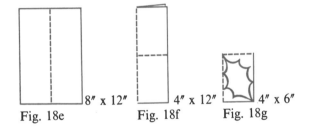

8″ x 12″	4″ x 12″	4″ x 6″
Fig. 18e	Fig. 18f	Fig. 18g

Conclusion

Makes a lovely table decoration. Encourage
children to take home and use project as
centerpiece during meals or to make a small
prayer corner in their rooms, to remind them
to ask Jesus to bring His light and life to
many more people this Christmas.

Variation

To make an *Advent wreath*, take paper plate and
cut out center.

Use holly leaves around paper plate rim (as
above).

Make four candles and place around rim at equal
distances. (See candle project.)

Tie ribbon around each candle.

Project 19
Scratchboard

Motivation

How Jesus dispelled the darkness by His message
of light and love. How Jesus forgives us, even
when we make mistakes, as they are part of
our growing in Jesus.

How Jesus' light dispells darkness in our souls.
How His forgiveness takes away the darkness
that may temporarily cover the soul.

Sense experience: Read and act out the story
of the prodigal son or other stories of
forgiveness (film strips).

Materials

Cardboard or heavy drawing paper (white
construction paper)

Crayons, at least 12 colors including black
(cover work area well)

Pointed objects, such as ballpoint pen, hair clip,
paper clip, end of comb, dull scissors, keys,
etc.

Procedure

Cover paper with different colored crayons,
making sure entire paper is covered heavily
(waxy), leaving no paper uncovered. Use light
colors only, no black or brown. Shapes can be
irregular; no pictures, just color shapes.

Cover entire colored-in paper with heavy black
crayon so all colors disappear.

Note: Children get very excited by this. Use this
to point out how sin can cover up the good in
us.

Scratch out design with pointed object (details
and samples in Creativity Kit, filmstrip and
tape). Scratch out whole areas, leaving some
black background for contrast.

Design can be any Christmas symbol: candle,
crib, tree; symbol of repentance and love:
heart, cross; a whole story, as used in
motivation period.

Spray entire picture with fixative. (See section
on materials in introduction.)

Mount on bright-colored construction paper.

Conclusion

May be used as a parallel activity to spiritual
concept of forgiveness: that through prayer
and good works the light of Christ grows and
increases in us, so that others will see and
follow Jesus as well.

God's gifts to me

Section 3
Jesus is born to save me

Project 20
Christmas trees
Two- and three- dimensional

Motivation
Basic concept now extended to the actual birth of Christ.

Discuss and explain the symbols of Christmas decorations.

Light is necessary for life. At Christmas the light of Christ should bring us renewed life in Him.

God shares this great gift with us; that is why we should share with others.

The "Great Exchange" takes place. Help the children concentrate on what they can *give*, rather than just what they will *get*.

In sharing with others, the young Christian responds to God's love for him.

Sense Activity: Have a short ceremony of lighting the Advent candle or candles in the Advent wreath, with appropriate music and spontaneous prayer.

2-D tree
Materials
Green construction paper

Crayons, paste, scissors

Mixed construction paper for background if desired

Glitter; odds and ends of wool, ribbon, foil, silver or gold paper (any leftovers from previous projects)

Procedure
Take green construction paper and fold in half like a booklet (Fig. 20a).

Place crease on left side (as with heart project).

Draw half a tree with crayon (Fig. 20b). (Teacher may do this on the board.)

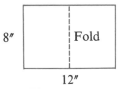

Fig. 20a   Fig. 20b

Cut out, holding top and bottom pieces of paper together.

Open and decorate.

Example: lights, balls, symbols, etc.

Draw outlines of decorations with white crayon for effect. Put paste on areas where you wish to sprinkle glitter.

Decorate both sides, if you wish to hang up trees, as in a mobile.

Paste tree down on a different-colored construction paper, if you wish to use it as a card or gift for parents. Draw under tree gifts or crib, etc., as desired.

Words or titles can always be added.

Variation
If cutting a tree is too difficult for very small children, use heavy yarns on oak tag or heavy construction paper.

Outline tree shape with heavy yarn (Fig. 20c). Draw or outline decorations with yarn. Fill in with macaroni and seed shapes (left over from earlier project). Add sparkle, or spray with gold.

Fig. 20c

3-D tree
Materials
Grade 3 & up

Green construction paper (two sheets for each child)

Paste, scissors, crayons, sparkles, (same as 2-D project)

Stapler

Paper plates or thin string (depending on what you do with it at the end)

Procedure
Follow steps in 2-D project for tree's basic shape.

Take second sheet of green construction paper and fold in half (same as first).

Place cutout tree shape (still folded in half) on top of second green construction paper, also folded in half. Make sure that crease of cutout tree is on top of crease of uncut paper (Fig. 20d).

Trace cutout shape of tree on uncut paper with pencil or crayon. It is essential for both tree shapes to be identical in size.

Cut second tree out, same as before.

Unfold trees and decorate as in 2-D project.

Staple or paste finished trees back to back *(crease against crease)* (Fig. 20e).

Fig. 20d   Fig. 20e

Conclusion

For mobile, staple a thin string to top of tree and hang.

For stand-up centerpiece, tape trees to paper plate. Decorate plates with glitter or paint, or spray with gold.

Snow spray applied lightly on trees is very effective.

End project with music and singing of Christmas carols.

Project 21
Tree decoration
For use in tree ceremony

Motivation

Help children to understand that there is more joy in *giving* than in *receiving* only. Plan a tree ceremony.

Tree ceremony: May be participated in by a small group of children of one or two grades, or by all grades in a large celebration to which parents may be invited. Can be held in classroom, auditorium, or church.

Materials

One fairly large *undecorated* tree

An Advent or Christ candle, or Advent wreath

Appropriate music (records or live)

Songs and prayers on mimeographed paper, if needed

Christmas decorations that the children have made and which they hold in their hands until the appropriate moment.

Procedure

Open with music and prayer.

Give a short talk or explanation of the purpose of the ceremony.

Individual children chosen from the group should light the Christ candle or Advent wreath candles, each child asking God that His great gift of His Son may bear fruit in us and in the world.

Each child brings his ornament to the tree and places it on the tree. (Older children may assist younger ones if necessary.) Each ornament bears the child's name and what he wishes to give to Jesus.

Parents are invited to join in. (Have a few extra ornaments on hand on which parents can write their own names and gifts.)

When tree is decorated, children can act out the gospel story (or read it) of Jesus' birth.

End with carols and refreshments, if desired.

Note: If all grades participate, each group can prepare something different to recite or perform at the end as a "gift" for Jesus.

Tree ornaments
All grades

Materials

Mixed colored construction paper

Markers, crayons, scissors

Paste, glitter, odds and ends

Procedure

Trace large circle on construction paper. (Use bottom of can or any round lid for tracing.) Cut out.

Decorate with markers, crayons (on one side only if used for tree ceremony).

Paste areas where glitter is to be used.

Yarn can be used to outline shape, if desired.

Back of circle: Child writes own name (paste and sparkle on name make it more festive). If used for ceremony, child may write in pencil something he will do for Jesus as a gift.

Examples: Do my homework, help mother, share toys, etc.

Staple a short piece of string to circle so it can be hung on tree.

Variations

Grade 3 & up

Instead of circle, other shapes may be used, such as:

Stars: Draw triangle right side up. Draw second triangle upside down on top of first (Fig. 21a).

Bells: Upside down U with an ellipse where opening is (Fig. 21b).

Light shapes: Enlarged flame shape (Fig. 21c). (See Project 18.)

Fig. 21a   Fig. 21b   Fig. 21c

Conclusion

Use in tree ceremony or let children hang ornaments on their trees at home.

Paper plate tree for wall

Motivation

Same as for Project 21

Materials

Grades 1-3

Paper plates (plain white)

Crayons, markers or paints

Scissors, tape, paste

Glitter, odds and ends

Procedure

One paper plate to each child.

Draw or paint a picture in the middle of the plate. Fill entire circle area with heavy crayon, marker or paint.

Examples: tree, Christmas scene, bells, candles, etc.

Color edge of plate with bright colors.

Put paste on edge and areas inside (sparingly in center) where sparkle is desired. Use different colored sparkles.

Cut small triangles all around edge of plate, to give it a star effect. (See Fig. 22a.)

Select a large wall area in room or hallway.

Arrange the plates in a form of a large Christmas tree by taping backs of plates to wall. Start with one plate as high as you can reach. Next row, two plates, next row three, increase gradually until triangle form of a tree is formed by plates. (See Fig. 22b.)

Fig. 22a   Fig. 22b

Add a stem part to triangle with plates or gold paper.

Add a separate paper for message of joy (preferably written by children).

Wall Christmas tree of triangles
Suitable for very young children

Materials
Colored construction paper, green and red only
Scissors, markers, crayons.

Procedure
Cut out large triangles (as in Project 16).
Decorate with drawings, colored paper, glitter, odds and ends.
Paste on large, light-colored background in this manner: Alternate colors, pasting one triangle right side up, next triangle up side down (Fig. 22c). To form large triangle, proceed as with plates.

Fig. 22c

Note: will give a festive checkerboard effect on wall.

Project 23
Christmas wreath
2-3 periods needed

Motivation
Same as Project 21

Seed wreath
Grades 1 & 2

Materials
Paper plates (simple white)
Scissors and paste
Assorted macaroni, pasta, seeds (as for name medallions)
Ribbon or heavy yarn
Glitter, stapler
Gold spray

Procedure
Period 1
Cut center circle out of plate.
Note: Teacher may precut this for the very young. Keep inner circle, it may be used for tree ornament or mobile.
Put assorted pasta into cups or box tops.
Paste is poured on rim of plate (a small section at a time) Seeds, macaroni, etc., are placed very close together on top of paste.
Note: Fill entire rim with the seeds and pasta. It is better to overcrowd than to have too little.
Let circle dry overnight.
Period 2
Repeat procedure on reverse side. Let dry overnight.
Period 3
Spray with gold paint.
Note: Should be done by teacher for very young so that spray does not go on children's faces.
Let spray dry (about ten minutes).
Add colored yarn or ribbon, if desired, or a little sparkle where touch of color is wanted. (Don't overdo glitter.)

Green holly wreath
Grade 2 & up
Materials
Paper plate
Ample green construction paper
Some red construction paper
Crayons or markers, scissors, paste, stapler
Red ribbon or yarn, silver or gold paper scraps if desired

Procedure

Cut center out of plate.

Fold green construction paper in half.

Keep folded and fold again, making a small area (one fourth of entire 8 by 12 inch paper).

Draw with chalk or crayon two fairly large holly leaves. (See Fig. 23a.)

Cut out, keeping paper folded. This will give you eight leaves. Repeat this as often as is necessary to form wreath.

Fold each leaf in half to give 3-D effect.

Paste one end of leaf to the brim of plate, two leaves at a time in V formation. One leaf pointing inward, one outward. (See Fig. 23b.)

Draw and cut out small red, silver, or gold circles.

Paste down at intervals, where leaves join in center.

Fig. 23a   **Fig. 23b**

Grade 3

Do only one side of paper plate. Spray other side with gold or silver, or paint green.

Upper grades

Repeat same procedure on reverse side of plate. Make sure leaves point in same direction on both sides.

Conclusion

All grades

Ribbon or yarn may be used to tie a bow at one side. Leave a small loop, so wreath can be hung on door, window, or wall.

Variations

Additional decoration can be made by older children for the center (the part that has been cut away). Candles, bells, stars, etc., may be cut out of light-colored paper and hung in the center, fastened by either tape or staples.

Project 24
Christmas figures

Motivation

Same as Project 21

2-D figures
Younger children

Materials

Paint, chalks

Individual paper or long shelf paper for mural

Paste, sparkle, gold and silver leftovers

Procedure

See section on painting and chalk, basic setup.

Discuss the figures of the Christmas story. Dwell especially on lesser known figures, such as the three wise men bringing gifts, the shepherds bringing gifts, etc.

Suggest that child put himself into picture, bringing a gift as a symbol of his love for Jesus.

Paint directly on paper or let child draw figure with chalk, keeping figures large.

Note: no pencil or crayon, as it inhibits freedom of movement.

Conclusion

Mount individual pictures, and place around room or prayer corner.

If large paper is used, let each child paint a section. When complete, use it in prayer corner or as part of Christmas decoration.

Make sure each child contributes something.

3-D figures
Grade 2 & up

Materials

Paper tube from toilet paper or half of paper towel tube

Colored construction paper

Paste, transparent tape, staplers, scissors

Wool ends, sewing trim, glitter, ribbons, scraps of fabric (if available), or sheets from wallpaper sampling book

Markers and crayons

Procedure

Joseph, Mary, Shepherds, Kings

Cover cardboard tube with colored paper, foil, or material

Cut circle from cardboard for head, paste and staple to tube (Fig. 24a).
Note: If round head is desired, use styrofoam ball or make a ball out of crumpled paper covered by cloth, stick inside tube, fasten with tape. (See Project 28.)
Color in face with markers or crayons.
Paste paper fringe or wool scraps to head for hair.
Drape cloth piece or construction paper around tube as a robe (construction paper cut as in Fig. 24b).

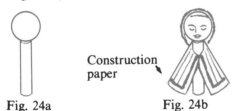

Fig. 24a   Construction paper   **Fig. 24b**

A strip of long colored paper folded in half the long way and stapled to back of tube extends forward as arms. Draw and cut hands, add to arms.
Add odds and ends, trims, and sparkle to dress up figure. Add details of who it is.
Examples: crown for king; staff for shepherd.

Variations

Baby Jesus
Same as above, but smaller tube is used.
Stuff a small white sock and tie off a section for the head. With thin thread or staples, fasten bottom of sock together. Add details with markers and trims.
Crib (simplest form)
Use a small cardboard box filled with straws or paper strips.
Make a small cut at bottom of box in each corner.
Cut four cardboard triangles of same size. Insert into cut slits, paste if necessary (Fig. 24c). If available, you could paste four empty spools to bottom of box.

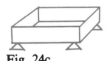

Fig. 24c

Clay figures
All grades — figure making

Materials
Soft clay, nonhardening for general use. (See section on material for hardening clay.)
4 sticks of clay to a child (if you use clayola)
Piece of wax paper for each child
Paper plate or piece of cardboard for each child
Paper towel or damp sponge for cleanup
Toothpicks, seeds, plastic forks, or other odds and ends.

Procedure
Discuss the people the children want to make, letting child enumerate as many specifics about them as possible.
Examples: Three wise men — clothing, transportation, gifts, etc.; size, age, movement of body.
Roll clay into ball. (See procedure under clay in Materials section.)
Form people, using odds and ends for texture and details of face and clothing.

Conclusion
Children may assemble figures on individual plates, boxes, or cardboard pieces or combine figures to form crib sets.

Project 25
Christmas windows
Grade 1 simplified form at end

Materials

    Thin white paper (parchmentlike airmail or
      typewriter paper)
    Rulers, pencils
    Markers (black plus several colors) or crayons
    Fixative spray

Procedure

    Draw a large simple picture of your choice. (Use
      pencil or black crayon only.) Use paper the
      long way. Do not draw too small or give
      details (Fig. 25a). Other ideas may be taken
      from Old or New Testament. Christmas
      symbols, bells, wreaths, candles may be used.

Fig. 25a

Superimpose vertical and horizontal lines at
    one-inch intervals with ruler and pencil or
    black crayon. For younger children use width
    of their rulers to simplify.
Go over all pencil lines with black marker (only
    outlines). If black crayon was used, be sure
    crayon lines are heavy, waxy, and sharp.
Color in each section outlined in black with a
    different color, using marker or crayon.
    Disregard the basic drawing.
Example: Dress may have different sections;
    feel free to use different colors.
Do not use the same color for adjoining sections.
    This gives a stained-glass-window effect.
Crayons should be pressed down hard to give
    waxy effect. (Markers are easier to use.)
Be sure entire paper is filled.
If necessary, go over black lines again at the end.

Conclusion

    Paste with transparent tape to window panes.
      Very effective when light passes through.

Variations

    Older children

May make larger designs for church doors or
    prayer-hall windows. Color both sides of
    paper, so that pictures can be seen inside and
    out. Paper may be trimmed and bordered
    with black paper for added effect.

Simplified procedure for very young children

Draw simple outline with black crayon or
    marker on white paper.
With ruler draw lines in any direction,
    crisscrossing basic design (not too many).
Color each section differently, keeping colors
    inside black outlines.

For all grades

If crayon was used, spray with fixative to avoid
    smearing.

Jesus is with us

Basic concept

Jesus is with us. He is our friend. To explore how Jesus' life here on earth showed us the way to the Father, we share in the love and friendship that exists between Jesus and His father by imitating Jesus in the way He lived here on earth. We grow in this friendship with Christ through knowledge of His Word left to us in the Bible and, through prayer and worship, learn to live and act like Jesus.

Project 26
Stick puppet

Motivation

Use one or more Bible stories (grade 1, one story only). Summarize and tell the children, or let them read a simple version of it (children's Bible or paperback series). Older children may read the stories themselves. *Always* relate story to their own lives. How would Jesus act today? How should I act?

Example: Take story where Jesus shows His concern for other people and takes care of their needs: wedding at Cana, Jesus calms the sea, Jesus heals the sick. Let children decide what part they would like to play.

Materials

Assorted colored construction paper
Scissors, paste, crayons or markers
Odd and ends
Flat or round stick (as for a balloon)
Tape

Procedure

Have each child take a sheet of light-colored construction paper (or drawing paper).
Fold in half and make a crease (Fig. 26a).
Open up like a book, cut on the crease of the two pieces, put one aside for later.

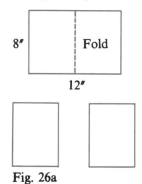

Fig. 26a

Place half of 8 by 12 inch paper the long way in front of you.

Draw with crayon a vertical line in the center from bottom of paper up to about the middle (Fig. 26b).
Cut only as far as the line is drawn.
Accordion pleat each leg (instructions on tape of Creativity Kit).
Take half a sheet of 8 by 12 inch paper for face.
Draw a large circle on it.
Cut out and paste on top of accordion pleated paper (Fig. 26c).

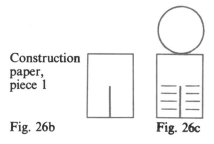

Construction paper, piece 1

Fig. 26b   Fig. 26c

Draw features with crayon or markers, or cut out features from colored construction paper.
Take leftover half of original construction paper.
Cut two long strips about one to two inches wide (Fig. 26d).
Note: Children tend to make arms and legs too short and skinny; encourage the size given here.
Accordion pleat arms.
Paste to side of body (shape shoulders).
Dress up the puppet according to the person it represents. Feet (double L, see Fig. 26e), hands (simplify to shape of mittens), and hair fringes may be added.

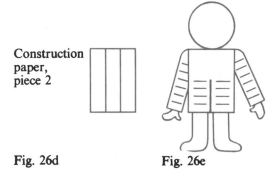

Construction paper, piece 2

Fig. 26d   Fig. 26e

Add odds and ends for decoration of dress and details.

Conclusion

Fasten finished puppet to stick with tape placed over stick and onto back of puppet. Stick should be long enough to be handled freely (about 20 inches). Use for playacting.

Project 27
Paper bag puppet

Materials
Small paper bag from grocery store
Markers or paints
Odds and ends of construction paper, wool, etc.

Procedure
Place paper bag with open end near you.
Fold at the bottom of the bag should be used
  for mouth. Half of mouth above fold, half
  below (Fig. 27a), so that when hand is inside,
  the movement of fold will simulate opening
  and closing of mouth.

Fig. 27a

Draw eyes and nose above fold with marker.
Add details of hair, eyebrows, etc., with odds
  and ends.

Conclusion
Hand is put inside bag, activating the fold.
Ready for playacting.

Variation
Paper-plate faces, more elaborately decorated
  and taped to a stick, may also be used for
  easy, quickly constructed puppets. (See mask
  project, Project 2.)

Project 28
Papier-maché puppet
Two periods

Materials
Paper bag
Newspaper, Elmer's glue (diluted in a coffee
  can: half water, half glue), cardboard tube,
  large size brush
Stockings (old ones from home)
Tape, paints or markers
Odds and ends of materials, felt pieces, wool,
  seeds, etc.

Procedure
Period 1
Stuff paper bag with newspaper to make a fairly
  good size head.
Insert open end of bag into cardboard tube.
Tape bag to tube, to make sure it is well
  connected.
Cover entire head with an old stocking (opaque
  or business sheer, for best results).
Tie tightly around neck part, cut off excess
  stocking.
Tape ends of stocking to tube.
Spread diluted glue with brush over entire head.
  Work in well so that stocking is tightly
  attached to newspaper.
Note: Work over newspaper area, and place wet
  head into a cardboard box for drying to avoid
  unnecessary mess.
Let dry for a day or more.
Period 2
Paint features on now hardened head base.
  (Older children might like to give the head a
  basic skin color first; if so, let dry before
  adding features.)
Paste wool ends, felt, seeds, etc., on head base
  for details of eyes, hair, etc.
Cut a poncholike dress out of material. (See
  Fig. 28a).

Fig. 28a

Insert tube into neck opening, tape around neck.
Sew up sides of dress. (Younger children may
  take it home and let mother help sew it up.)
Decorate dress with trims or draw on it with
  cray-pas.
Paste material or wool around neck to cover up
  tape.

Conclusion

Paper tube may either be cut off so child can put fingers inside puppet or be left on (for younger children) to be held like a stick underneath dress. (See sample in slides of Creativity Kit.)

Variation

Buildings for puppets

This is a great favorite with children of Grades 1-3. Each child may make a house for the puppet by using a cardboard box from the grocery store. Decorate it with colored paper or paint. A very large box may be made into a puppet theater.

Puppet theater: cut off bottom from large-size box. Place on a table. Use materials or paper for backdrop, curtains, etc.

Project 29
Colored chalks and paints

Motivation

Develop the theme of forgiveness. As a friend, Jesus understands when we make mistakes and is ready to forgive us, if we are sorry. Jesus encourages us to correct our mistakes, so as to please His Father. Discuss how wonderful one feels when one is forgiven.

Example: Story of the prodigal son.

Note: More explicit guidelines are given in tapes of Creativity Kit, concerning the child's need to express and manner of expressing moods and feelings.

Materials

Tables or floor space covered with newspaper

White drawing or construction paper

Large coffee cans half filled with water (place on paper plates to avoid mess)

Colored chalk broken in half (to facilitate handling); assorted colors in box tops or on paperplates

Paper towels and smocks are helpful for first experience with chalk. (Paint is optional.)

If paints are desired, use water color sets, with brush.

Procedure

After discussing the story and how it relates to life, let child decide what aspect of lesson he wants to draw.

Show children that the *point* of the chalk may be used for details but *also* that the *broad side* may be used for freer movement and color effect. Pressure on chalks creates variety.

Use chalk *dry* as well as *wet* (for wet, dip chalk into water).

Encourage mixing of colors or superimposing one or more colors.

Use fingers or brushes for mixing colors.

Build up colors to bright consistency.

If paints are used, use water color of same or different colors over dry chalk.

Use entire paper.

When filled up, put aside to dry.

Note: Children get very enthusiastic when working this way; encourage several drawings.

Conclusion

Finished drawings, when dry, can be sprayed with fixative to avoid smearing. (See section on materials.)

Mount and display.

OR Accumulate several drawings over a few lessons on a basic theme.

Examples:
   Jesus is my friend
   Jesus forgives me.
   Jesus is concerned about my needs.
   Jesus shows me the way to the Father
      through the Sacraments.
Collect several pictures, mount, and put together
   into a booklet with stapler.
Add prayers the children learned or made up
   themselves.

Project 30
Flannel board

Motivation
   Any of the above themes, Bible stories, or
   Sacraments.

Materials
   Assorted pieces of felt
   Sandpaper, scissors, glue
   Markers, crayons or cray-pas
   Piece of cardboard for each child (20 by 15
      inches) or large cardboard or plywood piece
      for group project

Procedure
   Draw basic shapes on felt with white chalk
      (fairly large).
   Cut out.
   Grade 1
   Use simple geometric shapes for body (Fig. 30a).
   Grade 3
   Child will use personal symbols and shapes for
      people. Do not expect or insist on realistic
      shapes at this age. Usual shape formed at this
      age level is shown in Figure 30b.

   Fig. 30a   **Fig. 30b**

(See tapes and slides in Creativity Kit for further
   guidelines.)
Assemble felt shapes, glue together when
   necessary.
Make as many different shapes as necessary. Add
   details of background.
Trace felt shape onto rough-grained sandpaper.
Paste sandpaper to felt (smooth side of
   sandpaper against felt).
Cover cardboard or plywood with large piece of
   dark felt. (Blue, green, grey are good basic
   colors.)

Conclusion

Cutout pieces can now be arranged and moved around on larger background piece to tell a story or describe an experience.

Note: Lettering can be done in the same fashion. When not in use, keep felt pieces in a shoe box. They can be reused many times to illustrate a story or theme or to develop a specific point of your lesson.

For younger children you might even like to develop a game. One person places the cut shapes on the flannel board, others guess what story is being told. The one who guesses correctly may in turn move the figures to make a new arrangement. A good way to recall previous lessons.

Project 31
Clay figures
3-D for all grades

Motivation

Let children act out attitudes using body movements.

Sense Experience: Express joy: arms outstretched above head or hands clapping. Express helping others, etc. Express prayer attitudes, etc. Make children conscious of the way they use their arms and hands, whether their bodies are stretched up or bent down, what legs are doing.

Materials

Nonhardening clay and clayola (comes usually in stick form, assorted colors; one box or four sticks to a child)

Paper plate

Ice cream sticks, tooth picks, or broken pencils.

Procedure

Roll clay into a large ball.

Knead the clay to make it soft and pliable.

Break off a medium-size ball for head, a large ball for body

Attach parts by pulling clay over the sides with finger. Make sure head is attached to body in this manner.

Pull out and push in the various parts of the face and body.

Example: Pull out the arms, legs, nose, etc.; push in for eyes, mouth, design on clothing.

Use sticks to make impressions or add texture. If body is very large, toothpicks can be used for support.

Decorate by pushing in seeds, leftover pasta shapes.

Arrange two or more figures on a paper plate.

Conclusion

Display.

Note: Older children might like to pool their figures into a group project, placing figures on a large cardboard or table, making background shapes out of clay or construction paper.

Example: the Christian community at worship.

In Jesus we have new life

Basic concept

Life must continually grow in order to remain alive. Build on the child's awareness of the new life that occurs in springtime to prepare him for the New Life he receives in Jesus risen. At Easter we celebrate the New Life that is offered to each one of us through Jesus' life, death, and resurrection. As with Christmas (Advent), a time of preparation is necessary in order to be more receptive for this New Life that is to be renewed in us each year (Lent).

Project 32
Seed drawing and seed collage

Motivation

Growth and change can sometimes mean struggle, like the little seed in the ground. But all is forgotten when new life appears, like the flowers, fruits, birds, etc. — all the signs of spring. I, too, must nurture the good in me, so I may live more fully in Jesus.

Sense Activity: Bring in different seeds, or let the children bring them in, to discuss the change that takes place when the seed is planted.

Example: Little apple seed becomes a tree.

Note: Playacting may be very effective here: Child makes believe he is a seed and slowly grows into a beautiful flower or tree. Detailed steps can be found in creativity tape.

Materials

Drawing paper
Colored chalk and paints
Seeds, paste

Procedure

Period 1

Let children draw and paint the story of a seed as acted out. (See tapes and slides in Creativity Kit.)

OR Let them draw and paint the different stages of growth, from a seed planted in the ground to a beautiful flower or tree.

Use color and chalk procedure from Project 29.

Period 2

Let the child draw and paint a picture of himself when he received the "seed" of faith in the Sacrament of Baptism.

Then show how he is growing in this faith through love and prayer and concern for others.

Seed collage and paint

Drawing 1

Paste a seed toward the bottom of the paper. Draw or paint what this little seed will be some day.

Drawing 2

Draw or paint yourself: how you will be a mature Christian some day and what means are at your disposal to help reach this goal.

Conclusion

If playacting "the growth of a seed" was used in the beginning of the lesson, a little prayer activity, asking to grow in Jesus' love, may be a fitting ending. The little prayer used earlier, "Lord, let me be that for which you have destined me," might be repeated, if desired. Or mount artwork and let the child write a little prayer of his own and attach it to the bottom of his painting. Display or use during prayer time.

Project 33
"New life" collage or mural

Motivation

Develop further the concept of "growth means change."

Sense Activity: Look at and discuss trees: how are they different in the winter and how do they change in the spring? Discuss other signs of spring.

Note: Several periods are suggested here for the entire art project. You can do part of the project (1 period) or all of it (3 periods), as desired.

Materials

For all periods

Large cardboard or shelf paper taken the long way for mural background

Paper or cardboard, 18 by 24 inches, for individual work

Assorted colored construction paper

Chalk or cray-pas

Scissors, paste, pencil

Trees

Period 1

Procedure

Show photos of trees in the winter, or look at a tree outside. Discuss how the branches look without leaves. (Grades 1 & 2 like to act out being trees.)

Draw a very large tree (only trunk and branches), using entire length and width of paper.

Chalk works best used the broad way (not point) for trunk. Point of chalk used only for twigs and smaller branches.

Spray with fixative.

Conclusion

Individual drawings are kept in folder. If mural is desired, let one, two, or more children repeat their drawings on the mural background, which has been taped to wall, floor, or large table. Spray; keep mural hanging up until next period. A poem about a tree may be a nice ending here.

Note: The bare tree with the sap asleep in the earth can be used as a symbol of us, in the beginning of our Christian life. As we add more things to the tree, they signify our growth as Christians, as followers of Jesus. At each successive lesson, add something to your tree (leaves, flowers, grass). It is most effective if you use one period for each of these additional signs of new life.

Leaves

Period 2

Materials

Crayons, paste, scissors

Procedure

Fold half a sheet of construction paper in half again.

Crease on the left side.

Draw half a leaf (Fig. 33a).

Crease

Fig. 33a

Cut top and bottom paper at the same time.

Repeat as often as you wish for individual project.

Color in, if desired, with different greens.

Paste into branches of tree drawn earlier.

Draw veins of the leaf.

Optional for mural: Write on back of leaf something you would like to do for Jesus until the next lesson. Each child pastes one leaf to a branch of the large tree (written part *not* showing).

Flowers

Period 3

Materials

Assorted colored construction paper

Crayons, paste, scissors

Procedure

Draw on half a sheet of colored paper a fairly large circle.

Draw petals in large half circles around center.

Color and cut out.

Paste to tree (same as for leaf).

Other additions can be made, such as:

Easter eggs

Easter bunnies

Grass, birds, etc. (See Project 39, New life mobile.)

Conclusion

New Life mural makes a lovely decoration for room or prayer corner. Individual projects should be displayed. This project should precede actual Easter projects, such as Easter eggs, bunnies, candles, etc.

Note: Entire project could also be used for banners with felt cutouts and yarn.

Project 34
Cross mosaic

Motivation

Jesus died forgiving us, who had hurt Him and caused His death. To die for someone is hard, but Jesus' death brought us life. So Jesus' death is sad because of our part in it, but joyful because Jesus was raised from the dead by God to give us hope in our own resurrection and a share in His life while we are still here on earth.

Sense activity: Find and look at pictures of crosses in the early part of history after Jesus' death (Ravenna Mosaics, jeweled crosses). Slides are available from libraries or museums. Discuss how artists tried to express both the joy and the sadness of Jesus' death. Show that the joy was the more dominant theme, expressed mostly by colors and symbols.

Materials

Construction paper (any color) for background
Assorted colored paper:
Use pages from wallpaper sample books. (See section on materials.)
Use scraps of gold and silver paper (leftovers from Christmas).
Note: Try to have a variety of textured paper as well as designs and colors (wallpaper).
Paste, scissors, glitter, odds and ends

Procedure

Fold one sheet of construction paper (background color) in half.
Crease, and fold again.
Open (crease should form a cross).
Use crease as guideline for cross.
Prepare mosaic pieces as follows:
Grades 1 & 2
Precut strips of paper about one inch wide and 10-12 inches long.
Grades 3 & up
Measure with ruler, draw strips about one inch wide and 10-12 inches long, cut strips apart.
Cut strips into one-inch squares; put into a box top or plate.
Paste is spread on the crease of background paper.
Squares are secured onto paste.
Finish one row at a time, add additional rows on either side of crease.
Grades 1 & 2
About three rows suffice, allow free choice of color, texture, and arrangement.

Grades 3 & up
Discuss and encourage forming designs by using alternate colors, alternate rows, etc.
Symbols and designs may be used for center of cross.
Draw with crayon fairly large, double lines to leave space for paper square.
Silver and gold can be used for accent, or as border.
Glitter, used sparingly, can be effective. (See samples in Creativity Kit.)

Variation

If preferred, seeds and pasted shapes can be used again, as for Christmas wreath project (Project 23). Mosaic technique can also be used for murals, other pictures, or words.
Examples: Last Supper, Jesus Is Risen, Alleluia, Easter Candle.

Conclusion

Projects can be displayed, mounted individually and taken home, or used for a large wall cross in hallway, or place of worship.
Note: Other projects on the theme of the cross are given in detailed guidelines and slides in Creativity Kit.

Project 35
Symbols of new life
Easter egg, tissue papier-maché

Motivation
Discuss how higher forms of life are born.
Example: birds.
Show pictures or filmstrip of how a baby chick is born. Relate the symbol of the egg to the Easter happenings, when Jesus comes out of the tomb alive. Jesus lives, therefore we may live.
Sense activity: Children crouch on the floor (lights out). They make believe they are baby chicks inside the eggs. At a given signal, children emerge from crouched position. Lights are turned on, and shouts of joy ("I am alive!") accompany the jumping up. This can be repeated, to imitate Jesus coming out of the tomb, with shouts of "Alleluia, He is risen!"

Materials
One balloon for each child
Crystal craft tissue paper, assorted colors
String, large coffee cans, Elmer's glue, thick brushes
Newspaper, paper towel, paper plates
Several cans spray starch
Spray shellac (one can for ten projects)

Procedure
Period 1
Inflate balloons to medium size, knot end or tie with string.
Dilute glue with water (half and half) in large coffee cans, one can for two to three children. Fill cans only half full.
Work area should be well covered with newspaper.
Provide paper plate, brush, and paper towel for each child.
Cut tissue paper into squares, about 5 inches on a side.
Each child only takes a few at a time (mixed colors).
Note: Select light-colored tissue paper only; avoid black, dark blue, purple, or brown (they are too opaque).
With brush, spread diluted paste over inflated balloon.
Press pieces of tissue paper onto wet surface of balloon. There is no specific order; just make sure the entire balloon is covered, except for a small section at the bottom where the balloon is knotted or tied and is held by the child.
Overlapping of colors is desirable.
After one layer is completed, spray with spray starch.
Repeat the procedure for a second and third layer while surface is wet.

Note: The paper-covered balloon tends to get a little soggy, but careful management can avoid unnecessary mess. Place wet balloon, after 3 or 4 layers of paper, glue, and starch, on a paper plate. Let dry.
Period 2
Dried balloons should be shellacked with spray or brush.
Several coats of shellac are desirable. Let dry.
With clay (self-hardening) or clayola, let children make one large baby chick or several smaller ones.
A small feather, if available, is inserted into wet clay for the tail.
Keep egg and clay figures on paper plate to dry.
Period 3
If balloons are completely dry, prick inflated balloon with a pin and remove, leaving only the tissue paper form.
Cut with scissors a jagged edge around the opening. (Enlarge the opening if necessary.) Spray the inside with shellac, if desired.
Paint baby chicks with poster paints (if self-hardening clay was used).
Paint and decorate plate, adding grass, flowers, ribbons, etc.
Spray shellac clay figures. Place in opening of the egg and glue down if you wish.

Conclusion
Papier-maché egg makes a lovely centerpiece and gift for parents.

Variation
Same technique can be used for flower shapes for older children or for puppet heads.

Project 36
Felt Easter egg

Motivation
Same as for papier-maché egg.

Materials
Felt squares of different colors
One piece of cardboard for each child
Scissors, Elmer's glue, white chalk
Cray-pas, trims, old stocking leftovers or cotton
balls for filling

Procedure
Draw on cardboard a large egg shape and cut
out.
Place cutout shape on top of felt piece, and
trace with chalk.
Repeat, so that you have two identical felt ovals.
Glue sides of felt pieces together, leaving about a
two-inch opening at one side.
Let dry.
While waiting, decorate egg with cray-pas, trims,
etc.
If time is limited, staple sides together to make
sure the egg won't fall apart when stuffing.
Stuff egg with stockings or cotton to a nice
plump shape.
Paste or staple together piece that was left open.
Paste gold cord around edge.
Tie bow at one end.

Conclusion
Makes a lovely pincushion for mother. If several
eggs are made this way, they can be used to
hang on an egg tree as a room decoration.

Variation
Get a large branch, with smaller branches on it,
from a tree or make a tree from unbent wire
hangers. Mix plaster of paris in a large coffee
can. Stick branch or hanger tree into wet
plaster of paris. Let dry (about one hour,
until firm). Decorate can with gift wrappings
or wallpaper, ribbons, glitter, etc. Hang felt
eggs from branches.
Note: This is especially suited for older
children, who like group projects.

Project 37
Blow paint egg tree

Materials
White or yellow construction paper
Black tempera (poster) paint (or India ink)
Cans or plastic containers
Straws (drinking straws), plastic spoon
Scissors, paste, glitter, wallpaper samples
Gold or silver paper

Procedure
Cover work area with newspaper.
Place a can or container with slightly diluted
black paint on table. (Two children to one
can. Older children could use India ink
instead of paint.)
With spoon place a puddle of paint on paper
(lower half of drawing paper).
With straws, blow paint upward, spreading to
upper part of paper (lifting paper slightly
from the table helps).
Design thus created will look like a tree or bush
in winter.
Note: Sometimes several attempts have to be
made until child gets the desired result.
Cut egg shapes from wallpaper, using different
colors, textures, and designs.
Paste onto the branches created by the blown
paint.
Decorate with glitter or trims.

Conclusion
Print a nice Easter text or greeting. It makes a
lovely Easter card.

Project 38
Easter bunny
2-D and 3-D

Motivation
Basically the same as for Easter egg. Relate the abundance of new life found in creation to the abundance of life we receive at Easter.

Materials
2-D, *paper or felt*
Light-colored construction paper or felt
Assorted colored construction paper or felt
Cotton balls, trims, odds and ends
Scissors, paste
Stapler, crayons, or markers

Procedure
For basic shape, draw on paper or felt one large circle for body. Draw on paper or felt one smaller oval for head.
Cut, and paste on colored background.
Draw and cut ears (same as leaves; Project 33).
Cut out and attach to head (Fig. 38a).

Fig. 38a   Fig. 38b

Arms and features can be cut out of paper or material or drawn with crayons or markers.

Variations
Cotton balls can be pasted inside paper shape, one next to the other, until entire bunny is made of cotton. Decorate with trims.
Felt gift: Paste bunny shape to felt, burlap, or cardboard background. Cut from felt a half circle as large as shape used for body. Paste this part over bottom half of bunny body. Paste only at the rounded edges, creating a pocket (Fig. 38b). Trim pocket with design or message. Finish off background so it can hang on wall. (See Project 14.)
3-D *bunny*
Basic shapes the same as for 2-D. Use double shapes, if it is to be stuffed. (See felt egg.)

Project 39
New life mobile
Flowers, butterflies, and birds

Motivation
Basically the same as for previous themes. Allow one period for each project.

Flower project
Materials
Paper plates, light color or white, small size tissue paper or crepe paper streamers (leftovers) scissors, paste

Procedure
Cut edges of paper plate in zigzag (see Christmas wall tree).
Spread paste rather thickly inside center of plate.
Cut small three-inch squares of tissue or crepe paper.
Ruffle together at center and bend in half. (See Fig. 39a.)
Place bent side into pasted area, making open ends stand up, creating a flower effect. (Fig. 39b)

Fig. 39a   Fig. 39b

Repeat as often as is necessary to fill entire center of plate. Make sure each piece is very close to the next. No spaces should be left open.
When finished, center should look like a tufted rug.
Color in edges with markers or crayons, or use glitter.
Note: For mobile, make two flowers of exact same size. Staple together, back to back. When finished, staple string at one end and hang.

Variation
If flower is to be used for wall decoration, or as a picture, make only one plate (suggested for Grade 1) and paste it to a background, or form a wall cross with it. (See Project 22.)

Butterfly project
Motivation
Show how a butterfly is born, the changes it goes through and relate to basic concept.

Materials

Assorted colored construction paper
Black construction paper
Paste, scissors, crayons or cray-pas, or markers
Trims of glitter, scraps of wallpaper, gold, etc.

Procedure

Take 1 colored paper, 9 by 12 inches, and fold in half.
Keep folded, with crease on left side.
Draw a butterfly wing, similar to heart shape done previously (Project 12). (See Fig. 39c.)

Crease
left

Fig. 39c    Fig. 39d    Fig. 39e

Hold both top and bottom piece together and cut out, careful not to cut on the crease, as indicated in Figure 39c.
Open and decorate wings with colored shapes, strings, glitter.
Take half a sheet of black, or dark construction paper (different in color than wings).
Draw body of butterfly. (See Fig. 39d.) Larger oval for body, small circle for head, plus antennae (make not too skinny or hard to cut).
Paste body, head, and antennae in the center of butterfly wings.
Note: Body should be as long as space between wings, so head and antennae protrude. (See Fig. 39e.)
Thread string through hole in body, or staple string to body. When hanging, make sure it can move freely.

Variation

If not used for mural, butterfly itself may be used as wall or window decoration, or part of a class mural.

Bird project

Motivation

Same as for Easter egg, Project 35

Materials

Assorted colored construction paper
Scissors, paste, odds and ends

Procedure

Fold 9 inch by 12 inch paper in half. Cut on the crease.
Take one half and fold again. (Keep second piece for later.)
Keep folded. Place in front of you with crease at top, away from you. (See Fig. 39f.)
Draw body and head of bird only on folded paper, making sure that head touches the crease and body fills rest of paper (Fig. 39f).
Cut out, holding both pieces together, careful to leave a small uncut section where the head touches the crease.
Take other half of sheet of construction paper that was kept aside.
Fold same as before, crease at top.
Cut strip about 2 inches from corner and as long as folded paper. (See Fig. 39g.)

  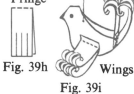

Crease at top   Fringe

Tail   Wings

Cut away
striped area
only.
Fig. 39f   Fig. 39g   Fig. 39h   Wings

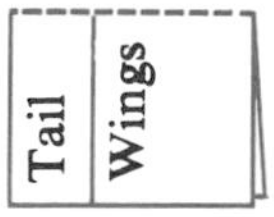

Fig. 39i

Fringe by cutting small strips about halfway up toward crease (Fig. 39h), so that strips are held together at the top.
Curl, roll each thin strip around a pencil or crayon, as far as the fringe permits. This will curl the paper.
Paste curled fringes to back of bird for tail. (See Fig. 39i.) End of bird should be inside fringed piece.
At the end of the bird where tail is to be attached, fold each side in about one half to three fourths of an inch. Insert folded ends into each side of the piece that forms the bird's tail. Paste both sides of tabs on bird's body to inside of tail piece (Fig. 39i).
Wings: Take leftover folded paper. Cut in half and repeat the same as for tail. Fringe and curl. Paste to either side of the bird's body (Fig. 39i). Attach string to back of bird, so it can fly. Decorate entire bird with crayon, glitter, or odds and ends if desired. (Do not overload.)

Conclusion

Each project is a lesson in itself and so can be used individually or as a part of a series, building up to a beautiful whole at the end.

THEME VI
The Christian life is life shared

Basic concept

Through Jesus' resurrection, Christians have become cocreators with God in building a better world. We must share the rich life that we have received in Christ with others. As we grow in the love of God, so we must grow in the love and concern for other men. In the way we live, and in the way we relate to other people, we manifest God's love for all human beings. By helping others to know and love God better, we share in the Mission of Jesus: to unite all people in the unity of the Father, the Son, and the Holy Spirit.

Project 40
Brotherhood: "I care" drawing and pasting

Motivation

Who is my brother? Who is my sister? Am I responsible for others? How much? Does it include all people? Discuss aspects of brotherhood, prejudice, discrimination. There is no place for these in the life of a Christian. Jesus died for all. Jesus saved all. We must act accordingly.

Sense activity: Look at magazine pictures or filmstrips of children of other races and backgrounds. List and discuss ways you can reach out to them, in your neighborhood, in your country, in the world.

Materials

Colored construction paper: yellow, shades of brown, white, light red
Scissors, paste
Crayons or paints

Procedure

Cut circles out of the different colored construction paper.
Paste on drawing paper. Avoid pasting them all in a row. Show how people in the foreground are closer to the lower half of paper and larger than people at a distance.
Draw or paint the rest of the body, showing where these people are to be found.
Examples: bus, playground, school, store, etc.
Show how the child relates to them.
Examples: giving a seat to an elderly lady; playing with children who are different than himself; helping carry a package.
Note: These are just suggestions that grew out of actual class participation. Let the children in your group come up with their *own* ideas, and do not tell them what to draw. Keep it practical on *their* level. (Situations and actions that are feasible for each child at his own age level.) See Creativity Kit slides for samples of children's work on this subject.

Conclusion

Mount and display. Let the children make a practical resolution to help someone else before the next lesson, and report on it to the class. Or plan, as a group, to visit someone sick or neglected.

Project 41
Brotherhood collage
Group project

Motivation

Basically the same as Project 40. Try to expand the children's concern to people they do not know personally, such as people in the community in which they live or the city, country, even the world (Grade 3 & up).

Sense activity: Find and cut out pictures from magazines of people of different races, walks of life, activities, and religious backgrounds.

Materials

Magazine with actual photos, not drawings; for example, *Life*, etc. (one magazine to a child)
Scissors, paste, crayons, markers
Colored construction paper, colored wool or string (optional)
Large piece of shelf paper or wrapping paper for group project

Procedure

Paste large paper to table, wall, or floor.
Divide group into smaller units of 3 or 4 children (depending on size of class).
Ask each group to look for something specific (about ten pictures in each category).
Examples:
Group 1: Children in need;
Group 2: Old people needing care;
Group 3: Handicapped or sick people of all ages, etc. (Grade 3 will expand this further than Grades 1 and 2.)
Give a time limit to search: about 15 minutes.
Each group chooses a leader who shows and discusses what the group has found.
Grade 3 & up
Let class decide on a form to paste pictures together on large background.
Example: a large outline of the world drawn with marker.
Paste pictures inside, overlapping and filling entire area. With marker or string outline parts of the world. Add symbols showing our unity in Christ.
Grades 1 & 2
Draw a large figure of Christ or a cross (only outline, no details).
Let children paste pictures inside shape, close together, overlapping.
Add symbols or words with markers or string.

Conclusion

Makes a lovely banner or background for closing ceremony.

Project 42
Holy Spirit mobile

Motivation

Find Scripture passages mentioning the Holy Spirit. Discuss the symbolisms used, for example, fire. Show the *good* properties of fire, how it warms and provides food, light, and strength. Fire is a source of power. (One child found his own symbolism, a rocket.) Show how the Holy Spirit is sent to us to strengthen us in the Spirit of Jesus: the spirit of Joy, Love, Peace, Strength, and Goodness.

Materials

Paper plate (one to a child)
Red construction paper, white or yellow construction paper
String (not too heavy)
Scissors, paste, markers, or crayons

Procedure

Make a hole with ball-point pen or pencil around the inner circle of the plate. For Grades 1 and 2, about four holes are sufficient; for Grades 3 and up, about seven holes, if desired.
Make one hole in the center of the plate. (See Fig. 42a.)

Fig. 42a   Fig. 42b

Fold red construction paper in half, make a crease.
Fold again and make a crease.
Draw one large flame. (See Fig. 42b.)
Hold paper folded together and cut out (will make four flames).
Make a small hole at one end of flame.
Staple or tie string to flame and to plate (outer circle).
Draw and cut a different symbol for the center hole, from white or yellow paper.
Examples: a dove, the world, or a figure of a person.
Note: If world shape is desired, it could be made from silver foil rolled into a ball.
Decorate with string.

Conclusion

Attach all shapes to the paper plate. Decorate plate with markers, crayons, or paints. Hang in classroom or take home. (For best results hang where there is a draft. Flames will move. Open up a paperclip to form an S. Attach one end to paper plate, the other end for hanging.)

Variations

If desired, each flame could have a word written on it describing a gift of the Holy Spirit, such as "Joy," "Peace," "Love," etc. If the symbol of the flame is not used, other symbols suggested by the children themselves can be used to describe how the Holy Spirit helps us to live more Christlike lives.

Project 43
My "I love Jesus" book
Several periods if desired

Motivation
How the spirit of Jesus helps us to be kind and loving with others. Summarize basic concepts that you have covered during the year.

Materials
Assorted colored construction paper
Crayons, markers or cray-pas
Odds and ends, if desired
(Use up leftovers)

Procedure
On each construction paper draw a picture of yourself.
Show how you can spread the spirit of Jesus to others during the summer months.
Staple sheets together, or make two holes on each sheet and pull through a ribbon or cord and tie (about five drawings; more if possible).
Include in booklet prayers and songs you have learned during the year.

Conclusion
Makes a good review project, as well as a useful reminder for vacation time. Can also be used for closing ceremony.

Project 44
A balloon happening
Two periods preparation

Motivation
Basically the same as previous projects for this theme. At the end of the school year we wish to share with others what we have learned. Discuss ways of modern communication. Our way: by balloon with a message.

Materials
Balloons: round medium size, about two to a child (in case of accident)
Helium gas (Look up in yellow pages. A safe container can be rented inexpensively.)
Thin colored paper, markers, crayons
String (thin) and stapler

Procedure
Period 1
Discuss what message you wish to send the people in your community (love, joy, peace).
Older children might like to include Scripture texts.
Draw message on thin paper strips, about 5 inches wide and 15 inches long. Decorate with drawings if desired.
Note: Do not make paper too heavy, or it will prevent balloon from rising.
Period 2
Fill balloons with helium. (Ask parents to help, if group is large.)
Tie balloon tightly with a string about 25 inches long. (Attachment comes with helium container — safe to handle.)
Tie inflated balloon to a chair or to child. Otherwise balloon will rise to ceiling. (Grade 3 & up may decorate balloons with markers.)
Attach paper strip with stapler or tape to the string, where it is tied to the balloon (Fig. 44a).

Conclusion
Prepare a short ceremony asking God that the message may reach many people and that they may receive the message in the spirit in which it is being sent. Invite other groups, parents, etc. Make it a community happening. Gather in an open place, like a schoolyard or town square. (Try to pick a slightly windy day.) Appropriate music can be played and sung.
Example: "Up Up With People."
At a given signal, release the balloons.
Note: This is a most effective and moving project in which adults as well as children enjoy participating. If you wish, stamp each message with the name of your group and hope for responses.

End of the year suggestions

Just as it was important to begin the year with basic introductory projects, so it is essential to give to the last lessons of the year a certain assurance of accomplishment. By that we do not mean to measure a child's progress in certain terms, but rather give the child the assurance and encouragement he deserves for participating in the religious program to the best of his abilities. A child's growth can be highlighted most effectively by a closing ceremony of some kind. Here, two kinds will be described, both involving each child to his capacity, as well as evoking participation on the part of the parent. This is important. In teaching the child the parents are indirectly affected all through the year. The more active this participation is, the better for the spiritual development of the child in the long run.

Art display

1. Have children bring in their art projects of the year, if they were not kept in a folder.
2. Try to select at least one project from each child.
3. Include class projects, like murals, mobiles, puppets.

Place

Select a room with much wall space or a hallway.

Mount

Individual projects should be mounted on larger colored construction paper, or several projects may be grouped on a larger cardboard. Attach to wall with masking tape, or make large cubes of cardboard and set cubes on tables.

Decorate

Decorate display room with banners, balloons, streamers, etc. Let the children help you put up artwork as much as possible. They take much pride and joy in this. Make posters or have invitations (made by the children) sent home to invite parents and friends.

Children can act as hostesses when guests arrive.

Time

Select a definite time period when all can come.

Optional

Combine art display with a short prayer ceremony, in which both children and adults participate, thanking God for the graces received during the year and asking Him to bless future efforts of growth in His knowledge and love. Certificates of promotion or some other tokens of the children's progress are appropriate here. Close with a party or refreshments.

Religious closing ceremony

Grades 1-3 *or all grades*

1. Have children and parents assemble in church or prayer hall.
2. Each grade (1-3) or all grades, depending on size of group, prepare an art project suitable for the occasion (projects made during year, or new ones).

   Examples:

   Grade 1 — flags, balloons

   Grade 2 — group collage, puppets, murals

   Grade 3 — banners, mobiles, collage, booklets
3. Each grade prepares either a prayer, a song, or petitions thanking God for the past year's blessing and asking for a safe and happy summer in the spirit of Jesus.
4. Art projects could be carried in procession, or placed around the room.
5. A short talk by a religious leader or teacher and the giving out of promotion certificates could end the ceremony on a solemn but joyful note.
6. The balloon happening described earlier (Project 44) could end the festivity outside the meeting place with a special flourish.

Optional art projects

May be used with any of the themes, or in addition to
projects selected for each theme.

Project 45
Clay painting

Materials
Nonhardening clay, assorted colors
Paper plates or cardboard
Toothpicks or broken pencils

Procedure
Roll clay into ball, knead to get soft texture.
Press a little at a time onto the cardboard. Push
down hard with fingers and spread (like finger
painting).
Colors can be mixed, built up to form a relief.
Toothpicks used for making designs or to add
details.

Use
For any theme, all grades (1-3 especially).

Project 46
Sponge painting

Materials
Drawing paper
Poster paints
Aluminum plates or plastic lids

Procedure
Place a small amount of paint on plate or lid.
Cut sponges into sections. Different sizes are
useful, but they should not be too small to be
easily handled.
Sponge is dipped into paint and freely dabbed
onto paper. Try different effects sponge
creates: spread, dab, twist, etc.

Use
Excellent for:
large overall patterns or designs;
freeing inhibited children in the early part of the
year;
interesting background fill-in for murals or
group projects;
fall tree or spring tree projects;
decorative additions to 3-D projects;
any theme, any grade.

Project 47
Crayon resist

Materials
Water color sets or poster paints
Crayons or cray-pas
Drawing paper

Procedure
Draw picture with crayon or cray-pas, pressing down hard to get waxy effect. Use light colors; white is effective for winter scenes.
Paint with darker colors over drawing, not only filling in background but actually painting over colored-in part as well. Paint will bead up, create interesting texture.

Use
Any theme, especially where you stress dark and light (Christmas) or life and death (spring).
All grades.

Project 48
Wood plaque

Materials
Wood scraps (lumberyard), size 8 inches by 12 inches, one for each child
Cray-pas
Gold spray (optional)
Fixative spray and shellac spray essential

Procedure
Make preliminary drawings on scrap paper first.
Transfer with white chalk or charcoal (not pencil) so mistakes can be corrected easily.
Color with cray-pas, pressing down for oil-painting effect.
Spray occasionally if build-up is desired.
Spray gold for background lightly.
When finished, spray with shellac several times, drying between times to a glossy finish.
Attach string or wire with staple gun to back of wood for hanging.

Use
Any theme or subject. Makes lovely gift for Christmas and Easter. All grades enjoy this (up to and including Grade 8).

Project 49
Wood sculpture
Two or more periods

Materials
Wood odds and ends of various shapes from lumberyard or from home (leftovers from buildings or hobby shops)
Elmer's liquid glue
Rubberbands of various sizes and strengths
Paints, brushes, shellac spray

Procedure
Period 1
Make quick general sketches of figures you want to make.
Keep shapes simple (Grade 3 & up).
Assemble shapes (Grades 1 & 2) and paste together, holding different sections with rubberbands, until dry.
Note: Needs a little patience; use this project toward end of year.
Period 2
When all pieces are assembled and paste is dry, paint with slightly thickened water paint or poster paint. (Thicken paint with soap powder.)
Add additional features with odds and ends: buttons, pasta, trims, glitter, seeds.
Shellac entire project a few times for glossy coat.

Use
Excellent for people figures (Christmas, Easter, Bible stories). Also animal figures; community projects of houses, churches, etc.

Project 50
Papier-maché
Grade 3 & up only

Materials
Buy shredded mix from any art supply store, or make it yourself.
To make: Shred newspaper, let soak overnight in mixture of flower and paste, keep moist in plastic bag.
Ready mix, which comes in powder form, is easily stored for ready use. Mix with water in large coffee cans to a thick paste only when children are ready for it.

Procedure
Used same as clay, but easily handled by very young. Dries more quickly than clay, is lighter and more versatile. Work on waxpaper or paper plate to avoid mess.
Keep moist while working, but not soggy.
Can be sanded down when dry and painted with paint or shellac.

Use
Any theme.